VIOLA

101 POPULAR SONGS

Available for
FLUTE, CLARINET, ALTO SAX, TENOR SAX, TRUMPET,
HORN, TROMBONE, VIOLIN, VIOLA, CELLO

ISBN 978-1-4950-9031-8

7777 W. BLUEMOUND RD. P.O. BOX 13819 MILWAUKEE, WI 53213

Visit Hal Leonard Online at
www.halleonard.com

CONTENTS

ABC

VIOLA

Words and Music by ALPHONSO MIZELL,
FREDERICK PERREN, DEKE RICHARDS
and BERRY GORDY

To Coda
D.S. al Coda
CODA

AFTERNOON DELIGHT

VIOLA

Words and Music by
BILL DANOFF

Moderately slow, in 2

To Coda
1.
2.
D.S. al Coda
CODA

AIN'T NO SUNSHINE

VIOLA

Words and Music by
BILL WITHERS

ALL YOU NEED IS LOVE

VIOLA

Words and Music by JOHN LENNON
and PAUL McCARTNEY

AIN'T TOO PROUD TO BEG

VIOLA

Words and Music by EDWARD HOLLAND JR.
and NORMAN WHITFIELD

ALL NIGHT LONG
(All Night)

VIOLA

Words and Music by
LIONEL RICHIE

ANOTHER BRICK IN THE WALL

VIOLA

Words and Music by
ROGER WATERS

AT SEVENTEEN

VIOLA

Words and Music by
JANIS IAN

BAD, BAD LEROY BROWN

VIOLA

Words and Music by
JIM CROCE

BIG GIRLS DON'T CRY

VIOLA

Words and Music by BOB CREWE
and BOB GAUDIO

BILLIE JEAN

VIOLA

Words and Music by
MICHAEL JACKSON

BRIDGE OVER TROUBLED WATER

VIOLA

Words and Music by
PAUL SIMON

CALIFORNIA DREAMIN'

VIOLA

Words and Music by JOHN PHILLIPS
and MICHELLE PHILLIPS

CARIBBEAN QUEEN
(No More Love on the Run)

VIOLA

Words and Music by KEITH VINCENT ALEXANDER
and BILLY OCEAN

CENTERFOLD

VIOLA

Words and Music by
SETH JUSTMAN

COPACABANA
(At the Copa)

VIOLA

Music by BARRY MANILOW
Lyric by BRUCE SUSSMAN and JACK FELDMAN

CRACKLIN' ROSIE

VIOLA

Words and Music by
NEIL DIAMOND

Moderately fast

1. 2.

Fine

D.S. al Fine
(take 2nd ending)

DO YOU BELIEVE IN MAGIC

VIOLA

Words and Music by
JOHN SEBASTIAN

DOWNTOWN

VIOLA

Words and Music by
TONY HATCH

DOWN UNDER

VIOLA

Words and Music by COLIN HAY
and RON STRYKERT

DUST IN THE WIND

VIOLA

Words and Music by
KERRY LIVGREN

THE FIRST TIME EVER I SAW YOUR FACE

VIOLA

Words and Music by
EWAN MacCOLL

EASY

VIOLA

Words and Music by
LIONEL RICHIE

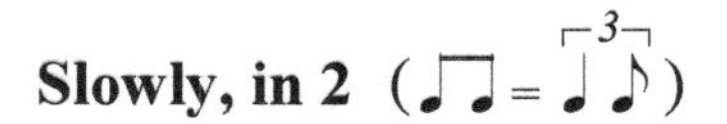

To Coda
1.
2.
3
D.S. al Coda
CODA

FREE BIRD

VIOLA

Words and Music by ALLEN COLLINS
and RONNIE VAN ZANT

GENTLE ON MY MIND

VIOLA

Words and Music by
JOHN HARTFORD

GIRLS JUST WANT TO HAVE FUN

VIOLA

Words and Music by
ROBERT HAZARD

GOD ONLY KNOWS

VIOLA

Words and Music by BRIAN WILSON
and TONY ASHER

GROOVIN'

VIOLA

Words and Music by FELIX CAVALIERE
and EDWARD BRIGATI, JR.

HAPPY TOGETHER

VIOLA

Words and Music by GARRY BONNER
and ALAN GORDON

HEY JUDE

VIOLA

Words and Music by JOHN LENNON
and PAUL McCARTNEY

I GET AROUND

VIOLA

Words and Music by BRIAN WILSON
and MIKE LOVE

I HEARD IT THROUGH THE GRAPEVINE

VIOLA

Words and Music by NORMAN J. WHITFIELD
and BARRETT STRONG

I SAW HER STANDING THERE

VIOLA

Words and Music by JOHN LENNON
and PAUL McCARTNEY

I STILL HAVEN'T FOUND WHAT I'M LOOKING FOR

VIOLA

Words and Music by
U2

I'M A BELIEVER

VIOLA

Words and Music by
NEIL DIAMOND

I WILL SURVIVE

VIOLA

Words and Music by DINO FEKARIS
and FREDERICK J. PERREN

1.
2.

IF

VIOLA

Words and Music by
DAVID GATES

IMAGINE

VIOLA

Words and Music by
JOHN LENNON

Medium slow

JESSIE'S GIRL

VIOLA

Words and Music by
RICK SPRINGFIELD

JUST ONCE

VIOLA

Words by CYNTHIA WEIL
Music by BARRY MANN

1.
2.

KARMA CHAMELEON

VIOLA

Words and Music by GEORGE O'DOWD,
JONATHAN MOSS, MICHAEL CRAIG,
ROY HAY and PHIL PICKETT

1.
2.

KILLING ME SOFTLY WITH HIS SONG

VIOLA

Words by NORMAN GIMBEL
Music by CHARLES FOX

LADY

VIOLA

Words and Music by
LIONEL RICHIE

LAY DOWN SALLY

VIOLA

Words and Music by ERIC CLAPTON,
MARCY LEVY and GEORGE TERRY

LEADER OF THE PACK

VIOLA

Words and Music by GEORGE MORTON,
JEFF BARRY and ELLIE GREENWICH

LEAN ON ME

VIOLA

Words and Music by
BILL WITHERS

LEAVING ON A JET PLANE

VIOLA

Words and Music by
JOHN DENVER

LET'S HANG ON

VIOLA

Words and Music by BOB CREWE,
DENNY RANDELL and SANDY LINZER

LET'S HEAR IT FOR THE BOY

from the Paramount Motion Picture FOOTLOOSE

VIOLA

Words by DEAN PITCHFORD
Music by TOM SNOW

LIKE A VIRGIN

VIOLA

Words and Music by BILLY STEINBERG
and TOM KELLY

THE LION SLEEPS TONIGHT

VIOLA

New Lyrics and Revised Music by GEORGE DAVID WEISS,
HUGO PERETTI and LUIGI CREATORE

LIVIN' ON A PRAYER

VIOLA

Words and Music by JON BON JOVI,
DESMOND CHILD and RICHIE SAMBORA

LOVE WILL KEEP US TOGETHER

VIOLA

Words and Music by NEIL SEDAKA
and HOWARD GREENFIELD

MANDY

VIOLA

Words and Music by SCOTT ENGLISH
and RICHARD KERR

MANEATER

VIOLA

Words and Music by SARA ALLEN,
DARYL HALL and JOHN OATES

MR. TAMBOURINE MAN

VIOLA

Words and Music by
BOB DYLAN

MONDAY, MONDAY

VIOLA

Words and Music by
JOHN PHILLIPS

Moderately

Fine

1.

2.

D.S. al Fine
(no repeat)

MONY, MONY

VIOLA

Words and Music by BOBBY BLOOM,
TOMMY JAMES, RITCHIE CORDELL
and BO GENTRY

MY CHERIE AMOUR

VIOLA

Words and Music by STEVIE WONDER,
SYLVIA MOY and HENRY COSBY

MY GIRL

VIOLA

Words and Music by SMOKEY ROBINSON
and RONALD WHITE

NIGHTS IN WHITE SATIN

VIOLA

Words and Music by
JUSTIN HAYWARD

NIGHTSHIFT

VIOLA

Words and Music by WALTER ORANGE,
FRANNE GOLDE and DENNIS LAMBERT

ONE MORE NIGHT

VIOLA

Words and Music by
PHIL COLLINS

Moderately slow, in 2

To Coda

1.

2.

D.C. al Coda (take repeat)

CODA

PHYSICAL

VIOLA

Words and Music by STEPHEN A. KIPNER
and TERRY SHADDICK

PIANO MAN

VIOLA

Words and Music by
BILLY JOEL

POUR SOME SUGAR ON ME

VIOLA

Words and Music by JOE ELLIOTT,
PHIL COLLEN, RICHARD SAVAGE,
RICHARD ALLEN, STEVE CLARK
and R.J. LANGE

REELING IN THE YEARS

VIOLA

Words and Music by WALTER BECKER
and DONALD FAGEN

RIGHT HERE WAITING

VIOLA

Words and Music by
RICHARD MARX

ROCKET MAN

(I Think It's Gonna Be a Long Long Time)

VIOLA

Words and Music by ELTON JOHN
and BERNIE TAUPIN

SAVING ALL MY LOVE FOR YOU

VIOLA

Words by GERRY GOFFIN
Music by MICHAEL MASSER

SHE DRIVES ME CRAZY

VIOLA

Words and Music by DAVID STEELE and ROLAND GIFT

SHINY HAPPY PEOPLE

VIOLA

Words and Music by WILLIAM BERRY,
PETER BUCK, MICHAEL MILLS
and MICHAEL STIPE

SILLY LOVE SONGS

VIOLA

Words and Music by PAUL McCARTNEY
and LINDA McCARTNEY

D.C. al Coda
CODA

SISTER CHRISTIAN

VIOLA

Words and Music by
KELLY KEAGY

(Sittin' On)

THE DOCK OF THE BAY

VIOLA

Words and Music by STEVE CROPPER
and OTIS REDDING

SMOKE ON THE WATER

VIOLA

Words and Music by RITCHIE BLACKMORE,
IAN GILLAN, ROGER GLOVER,
JON LORD and IAN PAICE

SOMEBODY TO LOVE

VIOLA

Words and Music by
FREDDIE MERCURY

SON-OF-A-PREACHER MAN

VIOLA

Words and Music by JOHN HURLEY
and RONNIE WILKINS

1.
2.

THE SOUND OF SILENCE

VIOLA

Words and Music by
PAUL SIMON

STAND BY ME

VIOLA

Words and Music by JERRY LEIBER,
MIKE STOLLER and BEN E. KING

SWEET DREAMS
(Are Made of This)

VIOLA

Words and Music by ANNIE LENNOX
and DAVID STEWART

Moderately

SWEET HOME ALABAMA

VIOLA

Words and Music by RONNIE VAN ZANT,
ED KING and GARY ROSSINGTON

TAKE ME HOME, COUNTRY ROADS

VIOLA

Words and Music by JOHN DENVER,
BILL DANOFF and TAFFY NIVERT

To Coda
D.S. al Coda
CODA

THESE DREAMS

VIOLA

Words and Music by MARTIN GEORGE PAGE
and BERNIE TAUPIN

Moderately slow, in 2

Fine
1.
2.
D.C. al Fine

THROUGH THE YEARS

VIOLA

Words and Music by STEVE DORFF
and MARTY PANZER

TICKET TO RIDE

VIOLA

Words and Music by JOHN LENNON
and PAUL McCARTNEY

TIME AFTER TIME

VIOLA

Words and Music by CYNDI LAUPER
and ROB HYMAN

TIME IN A BOTTLE

VIOLA

Words and Music by
JIM CROCE

TRAVELIN' MAN

VIOLA

Words and Music by
JERRY FULLER

25 OR 6 TO 4

VIOLA

Words and Music by
ROBERT LAMM

UP, UP AND AWAY

VIOLA

Words and Music by
JIMMY WEBB

WE'RE NOT GONNA TAKE IT

VIOLA

Words and Music by
DANIEL DEE SNIDER

WHAT'S LOVE GOT TO DO WITH IT

VIOLA

Words and Music by GRAHAM LYLE
and TERRY BRITTEN

1.
2.

A WHITER SHADE OF PALE

VIOLA

Words and Music by KEITH REID,
GARY BROOKER and MATTHEW FISHER

WICHITA LINEMAN

VIOLA

Words and Music by
JIMMY WEBB

WITH OR WITHOUT YOU

VIOLA

Words and Music by
U2

YESTERDAY

VIOLA

Words and Music by JOHN LENNON
and PAUL McCARTNEY

Moderately, with expression

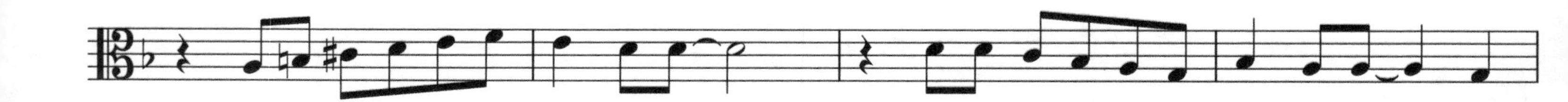

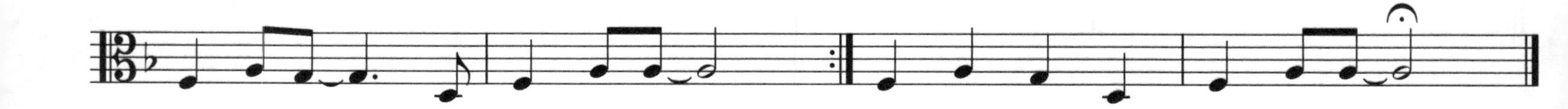

YOU ARE SO BEAUTIFUL

VIOLA

Words and Music by BILLY PRESTON
and BRUCE FISHER

YOU CAN'T HURRY LOVE

VIOLA

Words and Music by EDWARD HOLLAND JR.,
LAMONT DOZIER and BRIAN HOLLAND

1.
2.

YOU REALLY GOT ME

VIOLA

Words and Music by
RAY DAVIES

YOU'RE SO VAIN

VIOLA

Words and Music by
CARLY SIMON

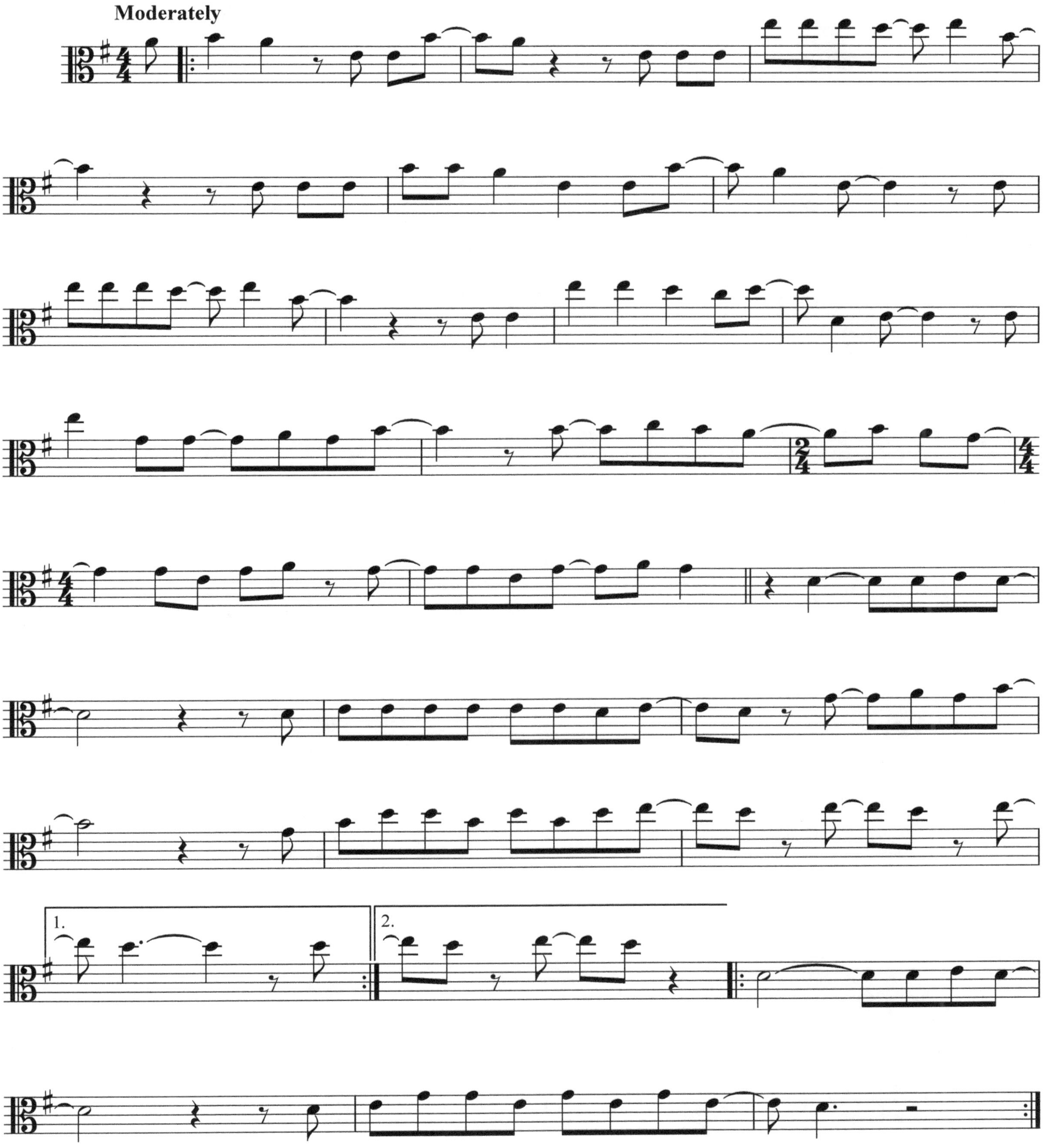

Moderately

1.

2.

HAL•LEONARD INSTRUMENTAL PLAY-ALONG

Your favorite songs are arranged just for solo instrumentalists with this outstanding series. Each book includes great full-accompaniment play-along audio so you can sound just like a pro!

Check out **halleonard.com** for songlists and more titles!

12 Pop Hits
12 songs

00261790 Flute	00261795 Horn
00261791 Clarinet	00261796 Trombone
00261792 Alto Sax	00261797 Violin
00261793 Tenor Sax	00261798 Viola
00261794 Trumpet	00261799 Cello

The Very Best of Bach
15 selections

00225371 Flute	00225376 Horn
00225372 Clarinet	00225377 Trombone
00225373 Alto Sax	00225378 Violin
00225374 Tenor Sax	00225379 Viola
00225375 Trumpet	00225380 Cello

The Beatles
15 songs

00225330 Flute	00225335 Horn
00225331 Clarinet	00225336 Trombone
00225332 Alto Sax	00225337 Violin
00225333 Tenor Sax	00225338 Viola
00225334 Trumpet	00225339 Cello

Chart Hits
12 songs

00146207 Flute	00146212 Horn
00146208 Clarinet	00146213 Trombone
00146209 Alto Sax	00146214 Violin
00146210 Tenor Sax	00146211 Trumpet
00146216 Cello	

Christmas Songs
12 songs

00146855 Flute	00146863 Horn
00146858 Clarinet	00146864 Trombone
00146859 Alto Sax	00146866 Violin
00146860 Tenor Sax	00146867 Viola
00146862 Trumpet	00146868 Cello

Contemporary Broadway
15 songs

00298704 Flute	00298709 Horn
00298705 Clarinet	00298710 Trombone
00298706 Alto Sax	00298711 Violin
00298707 Tenor Sax	00298712 Viola
00298708 Trumpet	00298713 Cello

Disney Movie Hits
12 songs

00841420 Flute	00841424 Horn
00841687 Oboe	00841425 Trombone
00841421 Clarinet	00841426 Violin
00841422 Alto Sax	00841427 Viola
00841686 Tenor Sax	00841428 Cello
00841423 Trumpet	

Prices, contents, and availability subject to change without notice.

Disney Solos
12 songs

00841404 Flute	00841506 Oboe
00841406 Alto Sax	00841409 Trumpet
00841407 Horn	00841410 Violin
00841411 Viola	00841412 Cello
00841405 Clarinet/Tenor Sax	
00841408 Trombone/Baritone	
00841553 Mallet Percussion	

Dixieland Favorites
15 songs

00268756 Flute	0068759 Trumpet
00268757 Clarinet	00268760 Trombone
00268758 Alto Sax	

Billie Eilish
9 songs

00345648 Flute	00345653 Horn
00345649 Clarinet	00345654 Trombone
00345650 Alto Sax	00345655 Violin
00345651 Tenor Sax	00345656 Viola
00345652 Trumpet	00345657 Cello

Favorite Movie Themes
13 songs

00841166 Flute	00841168 Trumpet
00841167 Clarinet	00841170 Trombone
00841169 Alto Sax	00841296 Violin

Gospel Hymns
15 songs

00194648 Flute	00194654 Trombone
00194649 Clarinet	00194655 Violin
00194650 Alto Sax	00194656 Viola
00194651 Tenor Sax	00194657 Cello
00194652 Trumpet	

Great Classical Themes
15 songs

00292727 Flute	00292733 Horn
00292728 Clarinet	00292735 Trombone
00292729 Alto Sax	00292736 Violin
00292730 Tenor Sax	00292737 Viola
00292732 Trumpet	00292738 Cello

The Greatest Showman
8 songs

00277389 Flute	00277394 Horn
00277390 Clarinet	00277395 Trombone
00277391 Alto Sax	00277396 Violin
00277392 Tenor Sax	00277397 Viola
00277393 Trumpet	00277398 Cello

Irish Favorites
31 songs

00842489 Flute	00842495 Trombone
00842490 Clarinet	00842496 Violin
00842491 Alto Sax	00842497 Viola
00842493 Trumpet	00842498 Cello
00842494 Horn	

Michael Jackson
11 songs

00119495 Flute	00119499 Trumpet
00119496 Clarinet	00119501 Trombone
00119497 Alto Sax	00119503 Violin
00119498 Tenor Sax	00119502 Accomp.

Jazz & Blues
14 songs

00841438 Flute	00841441 Trumpet
00841439 Clarinet	00841443 Trombone
00841440 Alto Sax	00841444 Violin
00841442 Tenor Sax	

Jazz Classics
12 songs

00151812 Flute	00151816 Trumpet
00151813 Clarinet	00151818 Trombone
00151814 Alto Sax	00151819 Violin
00151815 Tenor Sax	00151821 Cello

Les Misérables
13 songs

00842292 Flute	00842297 Horn
00842293 Clarinet	00842298 Trombone
00842294 Alto Sax	00842299 Violin
00842295 Tenor Sax	00842300 Viola
00842296 Trumpet	00842301 Cello

Metallica
12 songs

02501327 Flute	02502454 Horn
02501339 Clarinet	02501329 Trombone
02501332 Alto Sax	02501334 Violin
02501333 Tenor Sax	02501335 Viola
02501330 Trumpet	02501338 Cello

Motown Classics
15 songs

00842572 Flute	00842576 Trumpet
00842573 Clarinet	00842578 Trombone
00842574 Alto Sax	00842579 Violin
00842575 Tenor Sax	

Pirates of the Caribbean
16 songs

00842183 Flute	00842188 Horn
00842184 Clarinet	00842189 Trombone
00842185 Alto Sax	00842190 Violin
00842186 Tenor Sax	00842191 Viola
00842187 Trumpet	00842192 Cello

Queen
17 songs

00285402 Flute	00285407 Horn
00285403 Clarinet	00285408 Trombone
00285404 Alto Sax	00285409 Violin
00285405 Tenor Sax	00285410 Viola
00285406 Trumpet	00285411 Cello

Simple Songs
14 songs

00249081 Flute	00249087 Horn
00249093 Oboe	00249089 Trombone
00249082 Clarinet	00249090 Violin
00249083 Alto Sax	00249091 Viola
00249084 Tenor Sax	00249092 Cello
00249086 Trumpet	00249094 Mallets

Superhero Themes
14 songs

00363195 Flute	00363200 Horn
00363196 Clarinet	00363201 Trombone
00363197 Alto Sax	00363202 Violin
00363198 Tenor Sax	00363203 Viola
00363199 Trumpet	00363204 Cello

Star Wars
16 songs

00350900 Flute	00350907 Horn
00350913 Oboe	00350908 Trombone
00350903 Clarinet	00350909 Violin
00350904 Alto Sax	00350910 Viola
00350905 Tenor Sax	00350911 Cello
00350906 Trumpet	00350914 Mallet

Taylor Swift
15 songs

00842532 Flute	00842537 Horn
00842533 Clarinet	00842538 Trombone
00842534 Alto Sax	00842539 Violin
00842535 Tenor Sax	00842540 Viola
00842536 Trumpet	00842541 Cello

Video Game Music
13 songs

00283877 Flute	00283883 Horn
00283878 Clarinet	00283884 Trombone
00283879 Alto Sax	00283885 Violin
00283880 Tenor Sax	00283886 Viola
00283882 Trumpet	00283887 Cello

Wicked
13 songs

00842236 Flute	00842241 Horn
00842237 Clarinet	00842242 Trombone
00842238 Alto Sax	00842243 Violin
00842239 Tenor Sax	00842244 Viola
00842240 Trumpet	00842245 Cello

HAL•LEONARD®

0122
488

101 TIPS FROM HAL LEONARD

STUFF ALL THE PROS KNOW AND USE

Ready to take your skills to the next level? These books present valuable how-to insight that musicians of all styles and levels can benefit from. The text, photos, music, diagrams and accompanying audio provide a terrific, easy-to-use resource for a variety of topics.

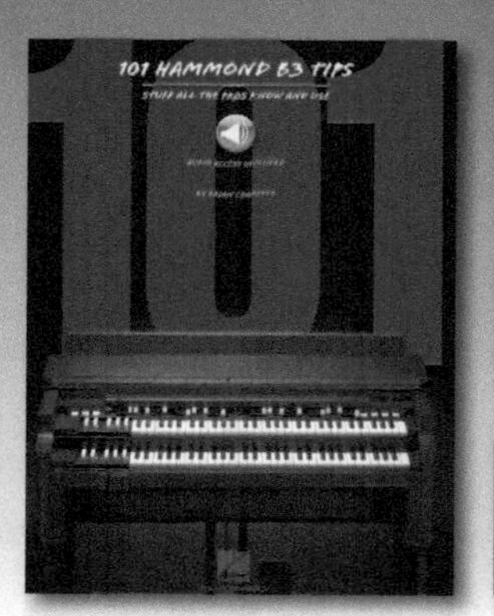

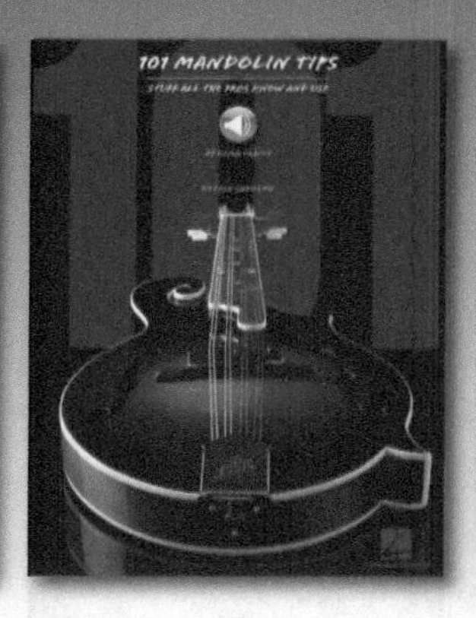

101 HAMMOND B-3 TIPS
by Brian Charette
Topics include: funky scales and modes; unconventional harmonies; creative chord voicings; cool drawbar settings; ear-grabbing special effects; professional gigging advice; practicing effectively; making good use of the pedals; and much more!
00128918 Book/Online Audio $14.99

101 HARMONICA TIPS
by Steve Cohen
Topics include: techniques, position playing, soloing, accompaniment, the blues, equipment, performance, maintenance, and much more!
00821040 Book/Online Audio $17.99

101 CELLO TIPS—2ND EDITION
by Angela Schmidt
Topics include: bowing techniques, non-classical playing, electric cellos, accessories, gig tips, practicing, recording and much more!
00149094 Book/Online Audio $14.99

101 FLUTE TIPS
by Elaine Schmidt
Topics include: selecting the right flute for you, finding the right teacher, warm-up exercises, practicing effectively, taking good care of your flute, gigging advice, staying and playing healthy, and much more.
00119883 Book/CD Pack.................................$14.99

101 SAXOPHONE TIPS
by Eric Morones
Topics include: techniques; maintenance; equipment; practicing; recording; performance; and much more!
00311082 Book/CD Pack.................................$19.99

101 TRUMPET TIPS
by Scott Barnard
Topics include: techniques, articulation, tone production, soloing, exercises, special effects, equipment, performance, maintenance and much more.
00312082 Book/CD Pack.................................$14.99

101 UPRIGHT BASS TIPS
by Andy McKee
Topics include: right- and left-hand technique, improvising and soloing, practicing, proper care of the instrument, ear training, performance, and much more.
00102009 Book/Online Audio $14.99

101 BASS TIPS
by Gary Willis
Topics include: techniques, improvising and soloing, equipment, practicing, ear training, performance, theory, and much more.
00695542 Book/Online Audio $19.99

101 DRUM TIPS—2ND EDITION
Topics include: grooves, practicing, warming up, tuning, gear, performance, and much more!
00151936 Book/Online Audio $14.99

101 FIVE-STRING BANJO TIPS
by Fred Sokolow
Topics include: techniques, ear training, performance, and much more!
00696647 Book/CD Pack.................................$14.99

101 GUITAR TIPS
by Adam St. James
Topics include: scales, music theory, truss rod adjustments, proper recording studio set-ups, and much more. The book also features snippets of advice from some of the most celebrated guitarists and producers in the music business.
00695737 Book/Online Audio $17.99

101 MANDOLIN TIPS
by Fred Sokolow
Topics include: playing tips, practicing tips, accessories, mandolin history and lore, practical music theory, and much more!
00119493 Book/Online Audio $14.99

101 RECORDING TIPS
by Adam St. James
This book contains recording tips, suggestions, and advice learned firsthand from legendary producers, engineers, and artists. These tricks of the trade will improve anyone's home or pro studio recordings.
00311035 Book/CD Pack.................................$14.95

101 UKULELE TIPS
by Fred Sokolow with Ronny Schiff
Topics include: techniques, improvising and soloing, equipment, practicing, ear training, performance, uke history and lore, and much more!
00696596 Book/Online Audio $15.99

101 VIOLIN TIPS
by Angela Schmidt
Topics include: bowing techniques, non-classical playing, electric violins, accessories, gig tips, practicing, recording, and much more!
00842672 Book/CD Pack.................................$14.99

Prices, contents and availability subject to change without notice.

HAL•LEONARD®

www.halleonard.com

THE ULTIMATE COLLECTION OF FAKE BOOKS

The Real Book – Sixth Edition

Hal Leonard proudly presents the first legitimate and legal editions of these books ever produced. These bestselling titles are mandatory for anyone who plays jazz! Over 400 songs, including: All By Myself • Dream a Little Dream of Me • God Bless the Child • Like Someone in Love • When I Fall in Love • and more.

00240221 Volume 1, C Instruments $45.00
00240224 Volume 1, B♭ Instruments $45.00
00240225 Volume 1, E♭ Instruments $45.00
00240226 Volume 1, BC Instruments $45.00

Go to **halleonard.com** to view all *Real Books* available

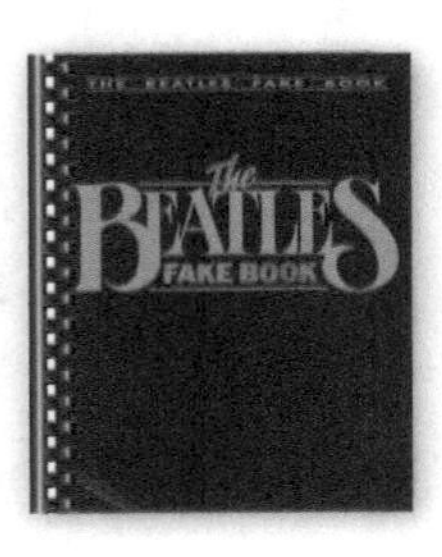

The Beatles Fake Book

200 of the Beatles' hits: All You Need Is Love • Blackbird • Can't Buy Me Love • Day Tripper • Eleanor Rigby • The Fool on the Hill • Hey Jude • In My Life • Let It Be • Michelle • Norwegian Wood (This Bird Has Flown) • Penny Lane • Revolution • She Loves You • Twist and Shout • With a Little Help from My Friends • Yesterday • and many more!

00240069 C Instruments $39.99

The Best Fake Book Ever

More than 1,000 songs from all styles of music: All My Loving • At the Hop • Cabaret • Dust in the Wind • Fever • Hello, Dolly • Hey Jude • King of the Road • Longer • Misty • Route 66 • Sentimental Journey • Somebody • Song Sung Blue • Spinning Wheel • Unchained Melody • We Will Rock You • What a Wonderful World • Wooly Bully • Y.M.C.A. • and more.

00290239 C Instruments $49.99
00240084 E♭ Instruments $49.95

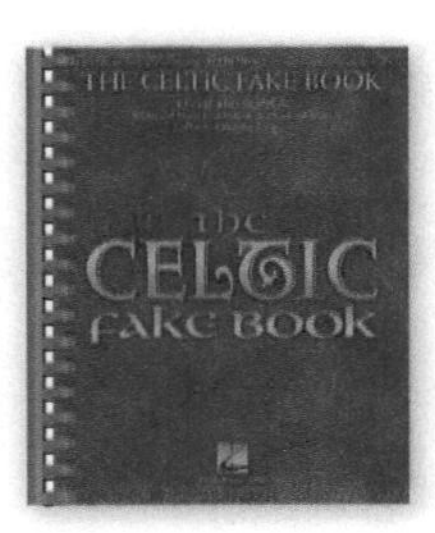

The Celtic Fake Book

Over 400 songs from Ireland, Scotland and Wales: Auld Lang Syne • Barbara Allen • Danny Boy • Finnegan's Wake • The Galway Piper • Irish Rover • Loch Lomond • Molly Malone • My Bonnie Lies Over the Ocean • My Wild Irish Rose • That's an Irish Lullaby • and more. Includes Gaelic lyrics where applicable and a pronunciation guide.

00240153 C Instruments $25.00

Classic Rock Fake Book

Over 250 of the best rock songs of all time: American Woman • Beast of Burden • Carry On Wayward Son • Dream On • Free Ride • Hurts So Good • I Shot the Sheriff • Layla • My Generation • Nights in White Satin • Owner of a Lonely Heart • Rhiannon • Roxanne • Summer of '69 • We Will Rock You • You Ain't Seen Nothin' Yet • and lots more!

00240108 C Instruments $35.00

Classical Fake Book

This unprecedented, amazingly comprehensive reference includes over 850 classical themes and melodies for all classical music lovers. Includes everything from Renaissance music to Vivaldi and Mozart to Mendelssohn. Lyrics in the original language are included when appropriate.

00240044 .... $39.99

The Disney Fake Book

Even more Disney favorites, including: The Bare Necessities • Can You Feel the Love Tonight • Circle of Life • How Do You Know? • Let It Go • Part of Your World • Reflection • Some Day My Prince Will Come • When I See an Elephant Fly • You'll Be in My Heart • and many more.

00175311 C Instruments $34.99

Disney characters & artwork TM & © 2021 Disney

The Folksong Fake Book

Over 1,000 folksongs: Bury Me Not on the Lone Prairie • Clementine • The Erie Canal • Go, Tell It on the Mountain • Home on the Range • Kumbaya • Michael Row the Boat Ashore • Shenandoah • Simple Gifts • Swing Low, Sweet Chariot • When Johnny Comes Marching Home • Yankee Doodle • and many more.

00240151 .... $34.99

The Hal Leonard Real Jazz Standards Fake Book

Over 250 standards in easy-to-read authentic hand-written jazz engravings: Ain't Misbehavin' • Blue Skies • Crazy He Calls Me • Desafinado (Off Key) • Fever • How High the Moon • It Don't Mean a Thing (If It Ain't Got That Swing) • Lazy River • Mood Indigo • Old Devil Moon • Route 66 • Satin Doll • Witchcraft • and more.

00240161 C Instruments $45.00

The Hymn Fake Book

Nearly 1,000 multi-denominational hymns perfect for church musicians or hobbyists: Amazing Grace • Christ the Lord Is Risen Today • For the Beauty of the Earth • It Is Well with My Soul • A Mighty Fortress Is Our God • O for a Thousand Tongues to Sing • Praise to the Lord, the Almighty • Take My Life and Let It Be • What a Friend We Have in Jesus • and hundreds more!

00240145 C Instruments $29.99

The New Broadway Fake Book

This amazing collection includes 645 songs from 285 shows: All I Ask of You • Any Dream Will Do • Close Every Door • Consider Yourself • Dancing Queen • Mack the Knife • Mamma Mia • Memory • The Phantom of the Opera • Popular • Strike up the Band • and more!

00138905 C Instruments $45.00

The Praise & Worship Fake Book

Over 400 songs including: Amazing Grace (My Chains Are Gone) • Cornerstone • Everlasting God • Great Are You Lord • In Christ Alone • Mighty to Save • Open the Eyes of My Heart • Shine, Jesus, Shine • This Is Amazing Grace • and more.

00160838 C Instruments $39.99
00240324 B♭ Instruments $34.99

Three Chord Songs Fake Book

200 classic and contemporary 3-chord tunes in melody/lyric/chord format: Ain't No Sunshine • Bang a Gong (Get It On) • Cold, Cold Heart • Don't Worry, Be Happy • Give Me One Reason • I Got You (I Feel Good) • Kiss • Me and Bobby McGee • Rock This Town • Werewolves of London • You Don't Mess Around with Jim • and more.

00240387 .... $34.99

The Ultimate Christmas Fake Book

The 6th edition of this bestseller features over 270 traditional and contemporary Christmas hits: Have Yourself a Merry Little Christmas • I'll Be Home for Christmas O Come, All Ye Faithful (Adeste Fideles) • Santa Baby • Winter Wonderland • and more.

00147215 C Instruments $30.00

The Ultimate Country Fake Book

This book includes over 700 of your favorite country hits: Always on My Mind • Boot Scootin' Boogie • Crazy • Down at the Twist and Shout • Forever and Ever, Amen • Friends in Low Places • The Gambler • Jambalaya • King of the Road • Sixteen Tons • There's a Tear in My Beer • Your Cheatin' Heart • and hundreds more.

00240049 C Instruments $49.99

The Ultimate Fake Book

Includes over 1,200 hits: Blue Skies • Body and Soul • Endless Love • Isn't It Romantic? • Memory • Mona Lisa • Moon River • Operator • Piano Man • Roxanne • Satin Doll • Shout • Small World • Smile • Speak Softly, Love • Strawberry Fields Forever • Tears in Heaven • Unforgettable • hundreds more!

00240024 C Instruments $55.00
00240026 B♭ Instruments $49.95

The Ultimate Jazz Fake Book

This must-own collection includes 635 songs spanning all jazz styles from more than 9 decades. Songs include: Maple Leaf Rag • Basin Street Blues • A Night in Tunisia • Lullaby of Birdland • The Girl from Ipanema • Bag's Groove • I Can't Get Started • All the Things You Are • and many more!

00240079 C Instruments $45.00
00240080 B♭ Instruments $45.00
00240081 E♭ Instruments $45.00

The Ultimate Rock Pop Fake Book

This amazing collection features nearly 550 rock and pop hits: American Pie • Bohemian Rhapsody • Born to Be Wild • Clocks • Dancing with Myself • Eye of the Tiger • Proud Mary • Rocket Man • Should I Stay or Should I Go • Total Eclipse of the Heart • Unchained Melody • When Doves Cry • Y.M.C.A. • You Raise Me Up • and more.

00240310 C Instruments $39.99

Complete songlists available online at **www.halleonard.com**